GW00724904

This Village I Know

A Play for Women

Tom Piggott

Samuel French – London
New York – Sydney – Toronto – Hollywood

© 1983 BY TOM PIGGOTT

This play is full protected under the Copyright Laws of the British Commonwealth of Nations, the United States of America and all countries of the Berne and Universal Copyright Conventions.

All rights, including Stage, Motion Picture, Radio, Television, Public Reading, and Translation into Foreign Languages, are strictly reserved.

No part of this publication may lawfully be transmitted, stored in a retrieval system, or reproduced in any form or by any means, electronic, mechanical, photocopying, manuscript, typescript, recording, or otherwise, without the prior permission of the copyright owners.

Rights of Performance by Amateurs are controlled by SAMUEL FRENCH LTD, 52 FITZROY STREET, LONDON W1P 6JR, and they, or their authorized agents, issue licences to amateurs on payment of a fee. **It is an infringement of the Copyright to give any performance or public reading of the play before the fee has been paid and the licence issued.**

Licences are issued subject to the understanding that it shall be made clear in all advertising matter that the audience will witness an amateur performance; that the names of the authors of the plays shall be included on all announcements and on all programmes; and that the integrity of the author's work will be preserved.

The Royalty Fee indicated below is subject to contract and subject to variation at the sole discretion of Samuel French Ltd.

> Basic fee for èach and every
> performance by amateurs   Code D
> in the British Isles

In Theatres or Halls seating Six Hundred or more the fee will be subject to negotiation.

In Territories Overseas the fee quoted above may not apply. A fee will be quoted on application to our local authorized agent, or if there is no such agent, on application to Samuel French Ltd, London.

ISBN 0 573 13320 4

ESSEX COUNTY LIBRARY

ER15159

CHARACTERS

Emily
Mrs Martha Belling
Mrs Grace Charrington
Mrs Bridges
Mrs Lizzie Ayrton
Mrs Gittins
Radio Commentator's voice (either "live" or recorded)

The action takes place in the lounge of a small country house on the fringe of a village somewhere in England

Time—the present

CHARACTERS

Emily. A servant in the twenty-five to thirty age group, who looks possibly older by reason of the hard, discouraging life she has been subjected to. Though in the denouement of the play she proves to be a woman of no mean talent, she never loses her servile manner. The portrayal is that of a personality that never quite surfaces; and her soliloquy (if such it might be called) at the end of the play conveys little of her triumph over circumstances and over her former oppressors. Throughout the action she is obsequious and almost diffident.

Mrs Martha Belling. Approaching middle age, but still quite attractive and certainly well groomed. A much more conventional type, but with a strong personality.

Mrs Grace Charrington. A contemporary of Mrs Belling, but weaker, more indecisive. Inclined to nervous apprehension but she can spark aggressively when roused.

Mrs Bridges. A domineering type with predeliction towards mannishness, even to shirt, collar and tie. A middle-aged, tweedy woman, loud of voice and extravagant of gesture. She rarely relaxes and spends much of her time on stage pacing to and fro.

Mrs Lizzie Ayrton. A giggly, inconsequential woman of around thirty-five; a satellite of Mrs Bridges, even though the latter plainly despises her.

Mrs Gittins. An elderly Cockney woman of considerable spirit and independence. She can be summed up as a rough diamond; and she is a likeable personality despite the evident local prejudice against her. When the occasion arises she succeeds without any apparent effort in dominating the scene, even over Mrs Bridges.

Radio commentator. Optionally a man or a woman; if a woman, the script can be read by one of the other characters, either "live" or recorded.

THIS VILLAGE I KNOW

The room is bright with french windows let into the rear wall, allowing a view of the garden. There is a door in the far corner L leading to the hall and front door. There is also a door R leading to another part of the house. The furniture consists of a settee and two easy chairs (see ground plan), and two high-backed chairs which stand like sentries on either side of the french windows. Against the wall L stands a table on which there is a transistor radio and a telephone. A fairly bulky manuscript has been tossed carelessly on to this table. The room should be dressed with lots of bric-à-brac and not show any particular taste

As the CURTAIN *rises Emily is standing with her back to the audience staring out through the french windows. The radio is tuned in to what is evidently a book review programme*

Commentator You will remember that in my weekly review of current books I invariably select what I think should be the book of the week. My choice this week happens to be the same as the Book Society's selection. They have chosen it as their "Book of the Month". You will recall that earlier in this programme I read some extracts from the new best-seller, "This Village I Know", whose author is an hitherto unknown writer. Her name is Mary Stalk, and she is to be congratulated on her immediate success. I think you will agree that the characters really do seem to come alive. Indeed, you get the impression that these are people who Mary Stalk knows personally; that they really *do* live in her village. Here we see the baser instincts of womanhood brought to the surface, and it would seem that they're a pretty mixed lot in this village. However hypothetical it all may be, the book is convincing, and I for one will await Miss Stalk's future work with considerable interest. Incidentally, her publishers tell me that she really does live in a village—somewhere in Wiltshire, I believe.

The telephone rings

And now to another promising new author ...

Emily crosses to the radio, switches it off and lifts the receiver

Emily (*on the phone*) Hello. Yes. Oh yes. No, she isn't. Miss Stalk isn't here. No she's away. No; I don't know how long. Yes; that's right; that's Miss Stalk. Yes, I've just been listening to it on the wireless. A message? Well, I'll try. Who? Who did you say? Hello. Hello. Oh dear! (*She replaces the receiver and idly picks up the bulky manuscript and flips through it aimlessly*)

The doorbell rings

Emily exits to answer the door

Mrs Belling (*off*) Good afternoon, Emily. I want to see Miss Stalk.

Mrs Belling enters followed by Emily

(*Purposefully*) I must see Miss Stalk. This is the third time I've called but each time all I hear is (*mimicking*) "Miss Stalk is busy ... Miss Stalk is not to be disturbed"... She can't be as exclusive as all *that*. Let me tell you, I've made up my mind to see this Miss Stalk, and you should know me well enough by now ...
Emily I was only saying what the mistress *said*, mum.
Mrs Belling (*settling herself on the settee*) Well, you can just go and tell her what I said.

Emily moves slowly and diffidently towards the door R

What kind of a woman is she anyway?
Emily She's—well—she's very nice, mum.
Mrs Belling She *must* be to write a book like that.
Emily Book? Oh, the book. I wouldn't know much about the book, mum.
Mrs Belling Why? Haven't you read it?
Emily Well, reading's hardly my line. I don't know ...
Mrs Belling No; don't suppose it is. Hard to say what *is* your line. You always *were* a bit footling. You can't even stay in a job for more than five minutes at a time. Worked for nearly everybody in the village, haven't you. And you end up here, with this—this Stalk woman. Why did you leave Mrs Bridges? Was it the same reason you left me—the same reason I got rid of you?

Emily Well, not altogether, mum. You see ...

Mrs Belling And why come here? Here of all places.

Emily Miss Stalk's been very kind, mum. She offered me this place, and she treats me very nicely too. And anyway, I've always liked this old house—ever since I came to the village from the orphanage.

Mrs Belling Bit above your station, isn't it—and a bit above Miss Stalk's too, I shouldn't wonder. What a thing! It's a downright shame what's come over this house. Things were a lot different when the Stewarts lived here, let me tell you. A gentleman, Mr Stewart was; a real gentleman. There were parties, and people coming and going—the gentry of the whole county. Gracious it was, and lively too. And *now* look at it. All chintz and lace and bits and pieces—no style, no taste, no nothing. As dead as a doornail. And a woman living in it turning out cheap novelettes. You didn't have to wait to see the Stewarts, no matter *how* busy they were. Gentlefolk don't *do* that sort of thing. And a lady doesn't either—not a *real* lady. Who *is* this Miss Stalk anyway?

Emily How d'you mean, mum, who is she?

Mrs Belling Well, who *is* she? Nobody's ever seen her; nobody's talked to her. Nobody around here had ever *heard* of her until she took this place and wrote this—this wretched novel. I ask you; who *is* she? What's she like? How old is she?

Emily Well, she's—she's sort of middle-aged, mum. She's—well, she's kind of homely like. Keeps to herself a lot, if you see what I mean.

Mrs Belling I'll say she does! Doesn't she ever go out? Doesn't she ever want to *meet* people? Nobody in the village has ever *seen* her.

Emily Well, when she isn't working she potters about in the garden a bit. She doesn't seem to *want* to go out.

Mrs Belling Then how does she get the material for her books? How can she write about people if she doesn't get to know them?

Emily Oh, I wouldn't know, mum. She seems to know an awful lot though.

Mrs Belling She does indeed! (*To herself*) A good bit too much.

Emily What did you say, mum?

Mrs Belling Nothing important. Now be a good woman and tell Miss Stalk I'm here.

Emily (*moving towards the door*) I don't think she'll like ...

The doorbell rings

Emily stops in her tracks, crosses to door L *and exits*

Mrs Charrington enters followed by Emily who closes the door behind her

Mrs Charrington Well, Emily, here I am. A couple of days you said and ... Oh, I see you've got company. I didn't expect to see *you* here, Martha.

Mrs Belling You're quite a surprise yourself, Grace.

Mrs Charrington Have you come to see Miss Stalk too?

Mrs Belling Well, I certainly didn't come to see Emily. You'd better sit down and make yourself comfortable. You may have to wait some time.

Mrs Charrington (*sitting in the easy chair* L) Yes, I know. Difficult to get hold of, isn't she. I've called two or three times, and each time ...

Mrs Belling So have I—and it's always the same story. Not in. Busy. Engaged. You'd think she was an MP or something.

Emily sits by the french windows. The other two women forget her presence.

Mrs Charrington Why are you here?

Mrs Belling M-m-m?

Mrs Charrington Why have you come to see Miss Stalk?

Mrs Belling And why *shouldn't* I come to see Miss Stalk? Is there a law against it?

Mrs Charrington No-o. Only ... (*She shrugs*)

Mrs Belling Only what?

Mrs Charrington I thought you might have some reason, that's all—some *special* reason.

Mrs Belling What could be so *special* about it?

Mrs Charrington Well, there's the book f'rinstance.

Mrs Belling Book? What book?

Mrs Charrington This book she's written—about the village.

Mrs Belling And why should I want to see her about the book?

Mrs Charrington Well, there's—there's quite a lot of talk in the village, that's all.

Mrs Belling There always is. What's it about *this* time?

Mrs Charrington It's—well, it's—it's hard to say, really.

Mrs Belling Apparently the villagers don't find it hard to say. What're you getting at, Grace?

Mrs Charrington Well, it's that bit about the Curate.

Mrs Belling Ho! So that's it! And just what're you suggesting?

Mrs Charrington Oh no, Martha dear; I'm not suggesting *any*thing. Only—only that's what they're talking about.

Mrs Belling And just *what* are they talking about?

Mrs Charrington Well, they're saying that that bit about the Curate and that—that woman in the book all seems to—well, all seems to add up.

Mrs Belling Add up to what?

Mrs Charrington Apparently it reminds them of Mr Hendon.

Mrs Belling Does it indeed! And who does the woman remind them of? *Me*, I suppose. Well, of course there's not an atom of truth in it. You know that, don't you?

Mrs Charrington Martha dear, I didn't think for a moment ...

Mrs Belling I made it perfectly clear at the time. There was absolutely nothing between Mr Hendon and me. And as for me leading him on—causing him to be moved away—well, it's too ridiculous for words! D'you think I've no respect for my husband and—and my home and—and friends and things? D'you think I've nothing better to do than chase after some parson who's young enough to be my son ...?

Mrs Charrington Martha dear, please! I never said you did. It's just that the villagers've got hold of this book and started reading things into it. You know how people gossip. It's all quite impossible really. An awful lot in that book just couldn't've happened.

Mrs Belling No? That's just it. *Is* it all so impossible? Tell me this. Why have *you* come to see this Stalk woman?

Mrs Charrington Wha-what; me? Well, I just wanted to meet her, that's all. I just thought—well—I just wanted to have a chat with her.

Mrs Belling A chat about what? I suppose it wouldn't be about those anonymous letters, would it?

Mrs Charrington Anon-anonymous letters? Good gracious! What a thing to say. I don't know what you mean.

Mrs Belling You know very well what I mean. Have you forgotten poor little Muriel Skilling—the wretched little Muriel they pulled out of the river after she'd tried to drown herself? Who was it wrote those—those filthy letters? Who was it turned the poor kid's brain? It wasn't *you* by any chance, was it? The book seems to suggest it *was*.

Mrs Charrington How can you possibly say such a wicked thing?

Mrs Belling *I* didn't say it. The book said it. And people who've read the book are saying it too. What's the name of the woman in the book? Harrington, wasn't it? Not much difference between Harrington and Charrington.

Mrs Charrington But that doesn't mean . . .

Mrs Belling Doesn't it? Not even when it describes you to a T? No, Grace; you can't fool me. I know why you're here. You came to have it out with this Stalk woman—p'raps find out just how much she knows.

The doorbell rings

    Emily jumps up and hurries off

Mrs Charrington Well, and what if I have? Yes. All right. I know what people are saying. But if it comes to that, you're here for the same thing—and it's no use denying it.

Mrs Belling Oh, I'm not denying it. I'm putting the law on her, and I'm telling her to her face; and I advise you to do the same.

    Mrs Bridges enters with a swagger. She positively dominates the room. She is followed meekly by Mrs Ayrton, and even more meekly by Emily

Mrs Ayrton comes to rest at Mrs Bridges' shoulder. Emily stands humbly and unnoticed by the door L *which she closes behind her*

Mrs Bridges Ah! And who have we here? Good afternoon, ladies. Come to pay your respects to our noted authoress? Quite a remarkable lady, isn't she!

Mrs Belling Er—Well, yes; she is. We—er—well, we just called like—just for a chat.

Emily (*still being ignored by the others*) I'll see if I can find Miss Stalk.

    Emily exits through the door R

Mrs Bridges How very nice! I hope it keeps fine for you. And have you brought gifts for her as well—a little frankincense and myrrh perhaps? Or *rat* poison?

Mrs Ayrton (*with a high-pitched giggle*) Rat poison! That's good *that* is!

Mrs Charrington Rat—rat poison? What on earth d'you mean, Mrs Bridges?

Mrs Bridges Don't be so naïve. You know very well what I mean. This is no friendly call you're making. This isn't any cosy little chat. You mean business. Both of you. And so do I for that matter.

Mrs Ayrton Yes; business; that's what it is.

Mrs Belling I can't see for the life of me what *business* we could *possibly* have.

Mrs Bridges No? Then what about the Parson scandal? Aren't you the Mrs Kelly in the Mary Stalk book? Have you forgotten the Reverend Michael Hendon you nearly got unfrocked? And what about *you*, Mrs Charrington—or is it Harrington? Remember the mystery of the anonymous letters? Has Mary Stalk solved the mystery for us, Mrs Charrington? Or is it all an amazing coincidence?

Mrs Belling ⎰ *(together)* Really! This is too much!
Mrs Charrington ⎱ I'll not have you saying such things!

Mrs Bridges Ladies! Ladies! Please! Let's be realistic for once, eh? I know very well why you're here. You needn't try to tell me it's all nice and friendly, because I know it isn't. You're here to have it out with her; to—to …

Mrs Ayrton To make it hot for her.

Mrs Bridges Shut up, Lizzie!

Mrs Belling *(to Mrs Bridges)* *You're* in the book too, aren't you?

Mrs Bridges Oh? Am I? And where do *I* come into it?

Mrs Charrington Cheating poor old Mr Bracewell out of his piece of land. Put him on the street you did; you put him out. You, with more land than you know what to do with.

Mrs Bridges Mrs Charrington, you talk too loud and too quick. Let's have some facts, shall we? In the first place, I never cheated *any*body out of *any* piece of land. That land was mine and always had been. Old Bracewell had it on lease, and when the lease expired … Well, that's all there was to it.

Mrs Charrington That's not what the book says. What the book says is you put him off the land after he'd done so much to *improve* it. The place was worth far more when you put him out. You couldn't've sold it for *half* as much if he hadn't been there.

Mrs Bridges Nonsense! What *is* this book anyway? A Bible or something? Has everybody gone crazy? Why've people got to take such a lot of notice of a cheap novel? It's nothing but an—an imagination run wild …

Mrs Ayrton That's right, that's what it is. Imagination run wild.

Mrs Belling Maybe; but people believe it just the same. And you're
as worried as anybody—for all your strutting and—and shout-
ing.

Mrs Ayrton *Who's* struttin' and shoutin'?

Mrs Bridges Shut up, Lizzie! Of course I'm worried. D'you think I
like being written about in a cheap novelette just like some—
some horror in an X film? 'Course I'm worried. But when *I'm*
worried I do something about it. You can be sure I'm not going
to let this Stalk woman get away with it.

Mrs Belling So; what *are* you going to do about it?

Mrs Bridges (*conspiratorially, leaning over the back of the
settee*) Listen to me. Doesn't anything strike you as odd about
all this? Who *is* this Mary Stalk? Have you ever met her? Has
*any*body ever met her? Have you ever even *seen* her? Has
anybody in the village ever seen her? How long has she been here?
Six months or so? Six months at the very outside—probably less.
Yet in that short time she's not only got to know everybody and
everything about them, but she writes a whole book about them
as well. D'you know how long it takes to write a book? Well,
months anyway—years p'raps. And how can she know all about
us when she hasn't even been outside her front door?

Mrs Belling It *is* peculiar, y'know, when you come to think about
it.

Mrs Charrington It's odd isn't it. What d'you make of it?

Mrs Bridges I tell you what *I* make of it. She's obviously got her
information from hearsay. From somebody in the village;
somebody in the know, and out to make trouble. And I think I
know who that somebody is.

Mrs Belling Who?

Mrs Bridges That Gittins woman.

Mrs Charrington Oh, not the old lady from London.

Mrs Bridges The old woman from London. That Cockney character. You read that book again carefully and see if I'm not right.
Apart from the Vicar and a couple of people who don't matter,
there's only one character in that book who gets off scot free. A
veritable saint she is—a heroine. And there's no mistaking the
description. It fits Mrs Gittins perfectly.

Mrs Belling *She's* no saint!

Mrs Ayrton No; *she's* no saint.

Mrs Bridges Don't keep butting in, Lizzie! I'm not saying she *is* a saint; but the *book* makes out she is.

Mrs Charrington A meddlesome old busybody—that's what she is. Not even a Christian. Never been inside a church door in her life. Not of her own accord anyway. She told me herself. "They carried me in to christen me", she said, "and they'll carry me in again to bury me."

Mrs Belling She's a hard woman all right. She's quite capable of that sort of thing.

Mrs Bridges A *very* hard woman. Born and bred in the East End of London like as not. She didn't want to come here in the first place, so I believe; and she's been letting everybody know it ever since. Something to do with her daughter wanting to get rid of her, shouldn't wonder. But she's the sort who comes and goes and finds out things. Doesn't *she* fit the part? Who else would have their knife into everybody? Who else would dare to talk like *she* talks? So, who else would tell Mary Stalk all this?

Mrs Belling Birds of a feather, if you ask me—this Stalk woman and herself.

Mrs Ayrton That's right—vultures, eh?

Mrs Bridges Maybe they *are* birds of a feather; but it's this Stalk character that interests me.

Mrs Belling I was asking Emily about her—before you came in ...

Mrs Bridges Emily! Don't talk to me about Emily. I should've listened to you in the first place about Emily. What a helpless nincompoop *she* turned out to be! Now I know why she walked out on me—to come here; to come and work for somebody who didn't know her. I wonder how long it'll take this Stalk woman to find her out—or p'raps she doesn't know any better.

Mrs Charrington That's true. Must be the last port in a storm for Emily. She's been everywhere else. I know. I was the *first* to get taken in. I was the one who took her out of that orphanage and gave her a home; remember?

Mrs Belling Oh, never mind about Emily now. Where is she by the way? (*She glances round the room*) It's Mary Stalk that matters. What're we going to do about her?

Mrs Bridges I think we've got a case against her—a court case— against both of them in fact. I'm told it could be slander and libel, both. We could have a case of slander against the Gittins woman,

and libel against Mary Stalk. Anyway, I've got my solicitors
working on it. Trouble is they need something to work on—
evidence—er—substantiation. Take a deal of proving, I'm
thinking. And yet, y'know, the proof *could* be there if we could
lay our hands on it. (*She begins pacing up and down thoughtfully*)

Mrs Ayrton Yes, it could, couldn't it.

Mrs Bridges F'rinstance, have any of you heard this story about
old Mrs Gittins rescuing a boy from the river? It's in the book,
remember?

Mrs Belling ⎱ (*together*) No; never.
Mrs Charrington ⎰ No. Not like it's in the book. Can
you imagine Mrs Gittins jumping in the river? Yes, I remember
that bit. Jumped in fully dressed and couldn't swim.

Mrs Ayrton *I* remember that. I remember saying to our Joe at the
time ...

Mrs Bridges You keep out of this, Lizzie.

Mrs Ayrton Well, she wrote about me too, didn't she? She wrote
about me trying to cheat the Post Office, didn't she?

Mrs Bridges And didn't you? Or did that allowance book fall out
of the sky? Anyway, don't interrupt. (*She pauses*) If only we
could *prove* something—something that really did happen.

Mrs Charrington I'm not sure I know what you mean.

Mrs Belling I think *I* do. What you're saying is—if one thing is true
it's *all* true.

Mrs Bridges Something like that, yes.

Mrs Belling But wouldn't we have to prove every single thing—
everything the book says happened? Seems to me that's asking
for trouble—especially when we're denying it. Take *me*
f'rinstance. It'd mean I'd have to admit to having a—a—an affair
with Mr Hendon, just to prove the truth of it. Not likely! Surely
it'd be far better if we all brought cases against her. You know, all
at once. We'd have a far better chance ...

During the following speech Mrs Gittins enters L, *obviously
surprised at the number of people in the room*

Mrs Bridges No; not subtle enough. I've already thought of that.
Smells too much like collusion—a sort of put-up job. Judges are
suspicious people, and juries—well, juries are just unpredictable.
I know; I've served on one. No; first of all, let *me* talk to Mary
Stalk. And then in due course ... we can *all* talk to her. (*She sees*

Mrs Gittins) Good gracious me! Where did you spring from? Mrs
    Gittins isn't it?

Mrs Gittins Sorry. Didn't mean to intrude I'm sure. I knocked
    once or twice, but nobody came so I tried the door. It was open so
    I—well, I just walked in. Didn't know there was anybody ...

Mrs Bridges So you just walked in! Just like that! How very
    informal of you. You just walked in—just like you always do, I
    suppose.

Mrs Gittins *Always* do? 'Ow d'you mean—always do?

Mrs Bridges Well, don't you? I should think you're part of the
    furnishings by now. Why should *you* knock? And anyway, it isn't
    a knocker; it's a bell. But why should *you* worry?

Mrs Gittins I 'ope you know what you're talking about. I'm sure *I*
    don't.

Mrs Bridges What I'm talking about is this—and you know very
    well. You're no stranger here *are* you?

Mrs Gittins I am y'know. I've never been 'ere before in me life—
    not *inside* the 'ouse anyways. Why? What it's all about?

Mrs Bridges Are you trying to tell us you've never been here
    before? How come you're a friend of Mary Stalk's then?

Mrs Gittins Friend? Friend of Mary Stalk's? But I'm *not* a friend of
    Mary Stalk's; never set eyes on 'er. What're you gettin' at?

Mrs Bridges Then why are you here? How can you just walk in like
    this without so much as by-your-leave?

Mrs Gittins 'Appened to be passin' an' I thought I'd drop in.
    Nothin' against that, is there? Matter of fact, I've just finished
    readin' 'er book. Very good I thought it was too.

Mrs Bridges No doubt you did; doesn't surprise me in the least.
    You recognized yourself, I suppose? Quite the little heroine,
    aren't we! Just a nice, quiet, old-fashioned lady who never does
    any harm to anybody.

Mrs Gittins What're you talkin' about? You tryin' to be rude or
    somethin'? What're you tryin' to say?

Mrs Bridges Mrs Gittins; listen to me. D'you know what's
    happened? Somebody amongst us has written a book. You say
    you've read it. All right; then you know all about it—except one
    thing that's probably escaped you. Let's hope that's the case
    anyway. But that book is about *this* village; and it's not only
    about this village but it tells all about the people in it. *I'm* in it; the
    Vicar's in it; Mrs Belling's in it (*indicating each in turn*); Mrs

Charrington's in it; Mrs Ayrton's in it; a whole *lot* of people're in it. And, Mrs Gittins, *You're* in it. In fact, you're the heroine. Most books, Mrs Gittins, have one hero—or one heroine—and one villain. But not *this* book! Oh, no! This one's got one heroine and a *hundred* villains. And I'm one of them; and she's one of them (*indicating each in turn*) and she's one of them. But you, Mrs Gittins, oh no. You're different. So how d'you account for it?

Mrs Gittins Account for it? What; me? Why should *I* account for it? *I* didn't write the ruddy book. Anyway, what's all this about me bein' in it? Where do *I* come into it?

Mrs Bridges Remember the bit about the old woman jumping in the river to save a boy?

Mrs Gittins What! That? That supposed to be me? Blimey; there's a turn-up for the book. Never jumped in a river in me life. Anyway I can't swim.

Mrs Bridges You mean you've never saved a little boy's life— anybody's life?

Mrs Gittins 'Course not. Not that way, anyway.

Mrs Bridges Oh, so you have done sometime.

Mrs Gittins Well, in the blitz I suppose I did—several times probably—me bein' in the civil defence an' all that. But what's *that* got to do with it?

Mrs Bridges And have you ever told anybody about it—this Mary Stalk f'rinstance?

Mrs Gittins What; about the blitz? No need; everybody knew.

Mrs Bridges No; about saving somebody's life.

Mrs Gittins 'Course not; nobody'd believe me if I did. Why?

Emily enters through the door R

Mrs Bridges We'll see why—but all in good time. Now Emily; at last. You'd better tell Miss Stalk to make up her mind. There're five of us waiting to see her and at least four of us are determined to stay until we have. Now get off with you!   ·

Emily All right, mum; but ... (*She speaks diffidently, finishing with a shrug*)

She exits through door R, *closing the door behind her*

Mrs Gittins I think you're a very rude woman. There's no call to talk to 'er like that; no call at all. It's not 'er fault. Poor woman's never 'ad a chance around 'ere—not with *any* of you. Just pushed around she's been—treated like dirt; and all because she's got no 'ome nor nobody to care for 'er.

Emily enters through door R. *She closes the door behind her and leans wearily against it. She no longer seems to care about the people in the room; her manner is one of resignation*

Mrs Bridges (*to Mrs Gittins*) I'll talk to you later. (*To Emily*) Well, Emily; where is Miss Stalk?

Emily (*flatly*) Miss Stalk isn't here.

Mrs Bridges   Not here?
Mrs Belling   } (*together*) But that's ridiculous!
Mrs Charrington   I don't believe it!

Emily No; she's not here. She never *has* been here. There never *was* a Miss Stalk.

There is incredulity all round as the women exchange glances, with the exception of Mrs Gittins who stares straight at Emily

Mrs Bridges Never was ... Good gracious me! Have you taken leave of your senses? What on earth're you talking about?

Emily No; there's no such person. You see, *I'm* Mary Stalk.

There follows a moment of silence while the significance of this pronouncement sinks in. Then everybody, with the exception of Mrs Gittins, starts talking at once

Mrs Bridges You must be mad. What're you saying ...?
Mrs Belling That's fantastic. It's—it's unbelievable ...
Mrs Charrington She's out of her mind! I always said ...
Mrs Ayrton She must be daft! Fancy saying a ...
Mrs Gittins Wait a minute! Shut up, the lot of you!

Everyone is silent

Emily d'you know what you're sayin'?

Emily Yes; of course I do. It's true.

Mrs Bridges This is utter madness!

Mrs Gittins Shut up! Let 'er 'ave 'er say. I've got a feelin' it *ain't* madness—far from it. Now listen, Emily. Tell us what happened. Never mind *us*; never mind what people may've done to you. Forget all that; see? Just remember this: *I* want to know; see? I want to know everything; so tell *me*. Just you take it easy. Relax. *I'll* see they don't crowd you.

Emily Well, it's true; like I said. *I* wrote that book. I wrote it because I *always* wanted to write it. I never knew I could write— not a book anyway. But I just started writing down what I knew, what I felt; and somehow it grew, and I finished what I wanted to say. I got the name of a firm—a publishing firm—out of the paper and sent the book to them; and a man came down to see me. He said they liked it. It wanted altering here and there, he said, but it was good and they wanted to print it. And that's how it happened. They never asked me if it was true; but it *was*. Most of it was. I know, because I was there when it all happened. I never made anything up. They put a few things in; like you—you jumping in the river; but all the rest was mine. When I bought this house, I . . .

Mrs Gittins *You* bought this house?

Emily Yes. I had a friend—the only real friend I ever had in my life. He used to visit the Home. That was before Mrs Charrington took me away and brought me to live here—in the village. He used to come and talk to us girls, and sometimes he'd take us out and give us little treats and things; I suppose he felt sorry for us. He seemed to take a liking to me—me in particular—said I reminded him of his own little girl who died when she was a kid. He used to bring me little presents and things, and I got to like him—more than anyone else I'd ever known. Then Mrs Charrington took me away. She said she'd give me a home, and I thought she was going to be a sort of mother to me. I thought I was going into a family and have a father and mother and relations and—and my own things for the first time in my life. But it didn't work out like that. All she wanted was a skivvy. I gave up hope then. I felt I didn't want to live any more. Later I left her and went to work for somebody else. I worked for *most* people in the village—those who could afford it; but nobody seemed to have any time for me. Just because *one* tried to put me down, they *all* tried to put me down; it seemed the right thing to do. And then, all at once, something happened. (*She pauses*) It was about six months ago. I was working for Mrs Bridges at the time. One day when she was out, a policeman called. He said he wanted to see *me*. He said some solicitors in London were trying to get hold of me. It was something about some money, he said. The old gentleman I'd known at the Home had died and left me some money. I didn't know it then, but it was about fifty thousand pounds.

Mrs Bridges		Fifty thousand!
Mrs Charrington	*(together)*	Oh my!
Mrs Belling		Oh dearie me!
Mrs Ayrton		Lot of money, wasn't it!

Mrs Gittins Go on, Emily.

Emily The solicitors were very nice to me. They asked me what I was going to do. I didn't know, so I stayed in London for a few days and thought it over. This house was up for sale because the Stewarts had moved away and nobody seemed to want it; but I'd always liked it, so I bought it. The solicitors said I got it cheap. I made them put it out that it was Mary Stalk who'd bought it. It was the first name that came into my head. I'd known a girl named Stalk at the Home. That's how the story got around about Mary Stalk. I came back, and then when the house was ready I left Mrs Bridges and came to live here. And then I got to writing, and—well, that's all there is to it.

Mrs Belling Well!

Mrs Bridges This is the most preposterous thing I've heard in my life!

Mrs Gittins I'm glad for you, Emily; real glad I am!

Mrs Charrington But it's not true; it *can't* be true!

Emily It's true all right.

Mrs Gittins 'Course it's true. Same's the book; that's true too.

Mrs Bridges True is it! We'll see about that! I don't care a damn if it was written by Emily, or Mary Stalk, or Rip Van Winkle. You'll pay for this. I'm taking you to court; and so are these other ladies. It's libel; that's what it is. Utter barefaced libel!

Mrs Gittins *(disparagingly)* Take 'er to court! You *do* that. And see where it gets you—right into the Sunday papers. 'Eadlines! Scandal! Take Emily to court and get 'er to tell 'em the facts. She *knows* the facts. She was livin' with you. *All* of you. Take 'er to court indeed! I 'ope you do. I can see it now—all across the 'eadlines. You'll be the laughin' stock of the whole country; despised; 'ated. Go on—sue and be damned.

Mrs Bridges Pshaw! I'm getting out of here. It's absolutely disgusting!

Mrs Bridges stamps indignantly out of the room via door L and Mrs Belling and Mrs Charrington, after a moment's bewildered pause, scramble to their feet and follow, with Mrs Ayrton trailing after them. Mrs Belling turns to say something, but she has to be content

*with an angry "Huh!" before she too disappears after the others,
leaving the door open*

Mrs Gittins An' good riddance to 'em!

Emily You don't think they'll try and cause trouble, do you?

Mrs Gittins Trouble? Not them! They're scared stiff. They're down
an' they'll stay down. This is the best thing that's 'appened in
years. I know it's taken twenty years off *my* life. P'raps from now
on this village'll be worth livin' in. "This Village I Know" will be
worth knowin'; eh? You know what it means, *don't* you. You'll
'ave to change the title now.

Emily Title?

Mrs Gittins Yes; you'll 'ave to change it to "This Village I *Knew*".
(*She pauses thoughtfully*) But there's somethin' worryin' me
about that book. That woman what jumped in the river. They're
sayin' it's supposed to be me.

Emily Well, what if it was?

Mrs Gittins She caught pneumonia, didn't she?

Emily nods quickly

Well, settle somethin' for me. Did I live?

CURTAIN

FURNITURE AND PROPERTY LIST

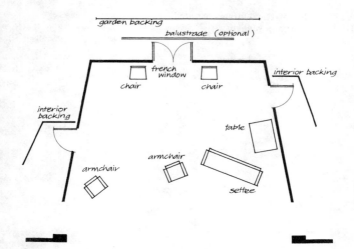

On stage: Settee
Two armchairs
Table. *On it:* transistor radio, telephone, manuscript
Two high-backed chairs
Dressing as desired

LIGHTING PLOT

A lounge. No practical fittings required
To open: afternoon sunlight
No cues

EFFECTS PLOT

MADE AND PRINTED IN GREAT BRITAIN BY
LATIMER TREND & COMPANY LTD PLYMOUTH
MADE IN ENGLAND